M000073825

THE
EVENING
RITUALS
JOURNAL

KELSEY LAYNE

A TarcherPerigee Book

WHAT DOES IT MEAN TO LIVE IN ALIGNMENT?

When we live in alignment, life feels effortless and
amazing. We feel a deep sense of inner peace,
profoundly connected to our inner being, and abundantly
happy. When we live in alignment, we make a conscious
effort to honor our inner voice and let it be our
guide in every decision that we make.

HOW DO YOU KNOW WHEN
YOU ARE LIVING OUT OF ALIGNMENT?

Did you know that whenever you feel stuck, unfulfilled,
confused, or lost it is often a sign that you are
living out of alignment with your true self?

We can find ourselves in this situation when we look outside of ourselves for all of the answers, make choices based solely on the opinions of others, or make decisions coming from a place of fear.

Sometimes this feeling of disconnect and unhappiness can feel as though it sneaks up on us gradually, and other times the discomfort is instantaneous. But we choose to stifle our inner voice and push forward, hoping for these feelings to disappear. Only they do not.

Following our inner voice is not always easy, but it is a muscle that can be strengthened. Once you practice this regularly, you will soon see how wonderful and happy your life has become, and your will to follow your intuition will expand.

Each weekday evening this guided journal will help you to reflect on your day by highlighting what made you feel happy and connected to yourself, serving as a reminder to integrate what makes you happy into your everyday life, if possible. It will also prompt you to uncover the root of any discomfort or unhappiness that shows up in your day and to then think about how you can start to turn the situation around.

This daily practice has helped me to create a life that I once only dreamed of, so I really hope that it brings as much joy to your life too.

DATE: / /

TODAY I FELT:

○ **IN ALIGNMENT:**

What brought me inner joy and peace today?

_____

_____

_____

_____

○ **OUT OF ALIGNMENT:**

Did I do something that I did not connect with or made me feel
unhappy? How can I start to change this?

_____

_____

_____

_____

TONIGHT I WILL FEED MY SOUL BY:

○ Learning something new   ○ Reading a book   ○ Getting creative

○ _____   ○ _____

TONIGHT'S MINDFULNESS PRACTICE WILL BE:

○ Yoga   ○ Meditation   ○ Exercise

○ _____   ○ _____

ALIGNMENT

 EQUALS

HAPPINESS

TODAY I FELT:

◯ **IN ALIGNMENT:**

What brought me inner joy and peace today?

_____

_____

_____

_____

◯ **OUT OF ALIGNMENT:**

Did I do something that I did not connect with or made me feel
unhappy? How can I start to change this?

_____

_____

_____

_____

TONIGHT I WILL FEED MY SOUL BY:

◯ Learning something new   ◯ Reading a book   ◯ Getting creative

◯ _____   ◯ _____

TONIGHT'S MINDFULNESS PRACTICE WILL BE:

◯ Yoga   ◯ Meditation   ◯ Exercise

◯ _____   ◯ _____

I AM DEEPLY CONNECTED TO MY TRUTH

TODAY I FELT:

○ **IN ALIGNMENT:**

What brought me inner joy and peace today?

_____

_____

_____

_____

○ **OUT OF ALIGNMENT:**

Did I do something that I did not connect with or made me feel
unhappy? How can I start to change this?

_____

_____

_____

_____

TONIGHT I WILL FEED MY SOUL BY:

○ Learning something new   ○ Reading a book   ○ Getting creative

○ _____   ○ _____

TONIGHT'S MINDFULNESS PRACTICE WILL BE:

○ Yoga ○ Meditation ○ Exercise

○ _____   ○ _____

Through

meditating

&

journaling

we can center ourselves and learn to easily
detach from the learned beliefs that do not serve
us, and in turn reconnect with our truth

TODAY I FELT:

◯ **IN ALIGNMENT:**

What brought me inner joy and peace today?

_____

_____

_____

_____

◯ **OUT OF ALIGNMENT:**

Did I do something that I did not connect with or made me feel
unhappy? How can I start to change this?

_____

_____

_____

_____

TONIGHT I WILL FEED MY SOUL BY:

◯ Learning something new   ◯ Reading a book   ◯ Getting creative

◯ _____   ◯ _____

TONIGHT'S MINDFULNESS PRACTICE WILL BE:

◯ Yoga   ◯ Meditation   ◯ Exercise

◯ _____   ◯ _____

I am in harmony with the present moment

TODAY I FELT:

○ **IN ALIGNMENT:**

What brought me inner joy and peace today?

_____

_____

_____

_____

○ **OUT OF ALIGNMENT:**

Did I do something that I did not connect with or made me feel unhappy? How can I start to change this?

_____

_____

_____

_____

TONIGHT I WILL FEED MY SOUL BY:

○ Learning something new   ○ Reading a book   ○ Getting creative

○ _____   ○ _____

TONIGHT'S MINDFULNESS PRACTICE WILL BE:

○ Yoga   ○ Meditation   ○ Exercise

○ _____   ○ _____

WEEKLY CHECK-IN

List this week's accomplishments no matter how big or small.

During a busy week, it can be so easy to forget all that you achieve. This could be anything from completing a chore to accomplishing something big.

✳ SACRED SPACE ✳

Reflect on your week, set intentions for the next, make notes, or free-flow journal.

TODAY I FELT:

○ **IN ALIGNMENT:**

What brought me inner joy and peace today?

_____

_____

_____

_____

○ **OUT OF ALIGNMENT:**

Did I do something that I did not connect with or made me feel
unhappy? How can I start to change this?

_____

_____

_____

_____

TONIGHT I WILL FEED MY SOUL BY:

○ Learning something new   ○ Reading a book   ○ Getting creative

○ _____   ○ _____

TONIGHT'S MINDFULNESS PRACTICE WILL BE:

○ Yoga   ○ Meditation   ○ Exercise

○ _____   ○ _____

I nurture my mind, body, and soul

TODAY I FELT:

○ **IN ALIGNMENT:**

What brought me inner joy and peace today?

_____

_____

_____

_____

○ **OUT OF ALIGNMENT:**

Did I do something that I did not connect with or made me feel
unhappy? How can I start to change this?

_____

_____

_____

_____

TONIGHT I WILL FEED MY SOUL BY:

○ Learning something new   ○ Reading a book   ○ Getting creative

○ _____   ○ _____

TONIGHT'S MINDFULNESS PRACTICE WILL BE:

○ Yoga   ○ Meditation   ○ Exercise

○ _____   ○ _____

FOLLOW YOUR OWN PATH

IT'S WHERE THE MAGIC HAPPENS

TODAY I FELT:

◯ **IN ALIGNMENT:**

What brought me inner joy and peace today?

_____

_____

_____

_____

◯ **OUT OF ALIGNMENT:**

Did I do something that I did not connect with or made me feel unhappy? How can I start to change this?

_____

_____

_____

_____

TONIGHT I WILL FEED MY SOUL BY:

◯ Learning something new   ◯ Reading a book   ◯ Getting creative

◯ _____   ◯ _____

TONIGHT'S MINDFULNESS PRACTICE WILL BE:

◯ Yoga   ◯ Meditation   ◯ Exercise

◯ _____   ◯ _____

4 Ways to Create a Mindful Morning

Note down an empowering affirmation

Take a walk or exercise in nature

Free-flow journal to gain clarity on your thoughts

Nourish your body with a healthy breakfast

TODAY I FELT:

○ **IN ALIGNMENT:**

What brought me inner joy and peace today?

_____

_____

_____

_____

○ **OUT OF ALIGNMENT:**

Did I do something that I did not connect with or made me feel
unhappy? How can I start to change this?

_____

_____

_____

_____

TONIGHT I WILL FEED MY SOUL BY:

○ Learning something new   ○ Reading a book   ○ Getting creative

○ _____   ○ _____

TONIGHT'S MINDFULNESS PRACTICE WILL BE:

○ Yoga   ○ Meditation   ○ Exercise

○ _____   ○ _____

NEVER
BE AFRAID TO
GO WITH THE
FLOW
OF YOUR OWN
ENERGY

TODAY I FELT:

○ **IN ALIGNMENT:**

What brought me inner joy and peace today?

_____

_____

_____

_____

○ **OUT OF ALIGNMENT:**

Did I do something that I did not connect with or made me feel
unhappy? How can I start to change this?

_____

_____

_____

_____

TONIGHT I WILL FEED MY SOUL BY:

○ Learning something new   ○ Reading a book   ○ Getting creative

○ _____   ○ _____

TONIGHT'S MINDFULNESS PRACTICE WILL BE:

○ Yoga   ○ Meditation   ○ Exercise

○ _____   ○ _____

WEEKLY CHECK-IN

What are you grateful for this week, and why?

Practicing gratitude has a number of benefits and can play a huge role in cultivating a positive mindset. But what makes this question even more powerful is the "why." The "why" helps you to delve deeper and discover what makes you truly happy.

✳ SACRED SPACE ✳

Reflect on your week, set intentions for the next, make notes, or free-flow journal.

TODAY I FELT:

○ **IN ALIGNMENT:**

What brought me inner joy and peace today?

_____

_____

_____

_____

○ **OUT OF ALIGNMENT:**

Did I do something that I did not connect with or made me feel
unhappy? How can I start to change this?

_____

_____

_____

_____

TONIGHT I WILL FEED MY SOUL BY:

○ Learning something new   ○ Reading a book   ○ Getting creative

○ _____   ○ _____

TONIGHT'S MINDFULNESS PRACTICE WILL BE:

○ Yoga   ○ Meditation   ○ Exercise

○ _____   ○ _____

SELF-LOVE AFFIRMATION

I AM
STRONG

TODAY I FELT:

◯ **IN ALIGNMENT:**

What brought me inner joy and peace today?

_____

_____

_____

_____

◯ **OUT OF ALIGNMENT:**

Did I do something that I did not connect with or made me feel
unhappy? How can I start to change this?

_____

_____

_____

_____

TONIGHT I WILL FEED MY SOUL BY:

◯ Learning something new ◯ Reading a book ◯ Getting creative

◯ _____ ◯ _____

TONIGHT'S MINDFULNESS PRACTICE WILL BE:

◯ Yoga ◯ Meditation ◯ Exercise

◯ _____ ◯ _____

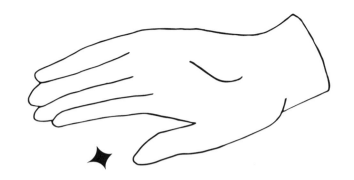

NEVER
LET YOUR
DREAMS
GO

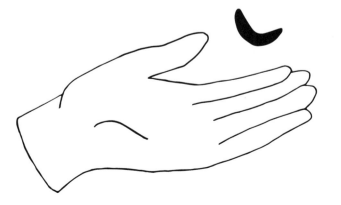

TODAY I FELT:

◯ **IN ALIGNMENT:**

What brought me inner joy and peace today?

_____

_____

_____

_____

◯ **OUT OF ALIGNMENT:**

Did I do something that I did not connect with or made me feel
unhappy? How can I start to change this?

_____

_____

_____

_____

TONIGHT I WILL FEED MY SOUL BY:

◯ Learning something new   ◯ Reading a book   ◯ Getting creative

◯ _____   ◯ _____

TONIGHT'S MINDFULNESS PRACTICE WILL BE:

◯ Yoga   ◯ Meditation   ◯ Exercise

◯ _____   ◯ _____

Self-Love

is actively treating yourself with the same love, kindness, and respect that you would give to those you love

TODAY I FELT:

◯ **IN ALIGNMENT:**

What brought me inner joy and peace today?

_____

_____

_____

_____

◯ **OUT OF ALIGNMENT:**

Did I do something that I did not connect with or made me feel
unhappy? How can I start to change this?

_____

_____

_____

_____

TONIGHT I WILL FEED MY SOUL BY:

◯ Learning something new   ◯ Reading a book   ◯ Getting creative

◯ _____   ◯ _____

TONIGHT'S MINDFULNESS PRACTICE WILL BE:

◯ Yoga   ◯ Meditation   ◯ Exercise

◯ _____   ◯ _____

✳ **MINDFULNESS AFFIRMATION** ✳

I ALLOW

all worries
to fade away ✳

AS I TRUST

my guidance
from within

TODAY I FELT:

○ **IN ALIGNMENT:**

What brought me inner joy and peace today?

_____

_____

_____

_____

○ **OUT OF ALIGNMENT:**

Did I do something that I did not connect with or made me feel
unhappy? How can I start to change this?

_____

_____

_____

_____

TONIGHT I WILL FEED MY SOUL BY:

○ Learning something new   ○ Reading a book   ○ Getting creative

○ _____   ○ _____

TONIGHT'S MINDFULNESS PRACTICE WILL BE:

○ Yoga   ○ Meditation   ○ Exercise

○ _____   ○ _____

WEEKLY CHECK-IN

What would you like to make more time for next week, and why?

✳ SACRED SPACE ✳

Reflect on your week, set intentions for the next, make notes, or free-flow journal.

TODAY I FELT:

○ **IN ALIGNMENT:**

What brought me inner joy and peace today?

_____

_____

_____

_____

○ **OUT OF ALIGNMENT:**

Did I do something that I did not connect with or made me feel
unhappy? How can I start to change this?

_____

_____

_____

_____

TONIGHT I WILL FEED MY SOUL BY:

○ Learning something new   ○ Reading a book   ○ Getting creative

○ _____   ○ _____

TONIGHT'S MINDFULNESS PRACTICE WILL BE:

○ Yoga   ○ Meditation   ○ Exercise

○ _____   ○ _____

I know myself

TODAY I FELT:

◯ **IN ALIGNMENT:**

What brought me inner joy and peace today?

_____

_____

_____

_____

◯ **OUT OF ALIGNMENT:**

Did I do something that I did not connect with or made me feel
unhappy? How can I start to change this?

_____

_____

_____

_____

TONIGHT I WILL FEED MY SOUL BY:

◯ Learning something new   ◯ Reading a book   ◯ Getting creative

◯ _____   ◯ _____

TONIGHT'S MINDFULNESS PRACTICE WILL BE:

◯ Yoga   ◯ Meditation   ◯ Exercise

◯ _____   ◯ _____

I AM

POWERFUL

TODAY I FELT:

◯ **IN ALIGNMENT:**

What brought me inner joy and peace today?

_____

_____

_____

_____

◯ **OUT OF ALIGNMENT:**

Did I do something that I did not connect with or made me feel
unhappy? How can I start to change this?

_____

_____

_____

_____

TONIGHT I WILL FEED MY SOUL BY:

◯ Learning something new   ◯ Reading a book   ◯ Getting creative

◯ _____   ◯ _____

TONIGHT'S MINDFULNESS PRACTICE WILL BE:

◯ Yoga   ◯ Meditation   ◯ Exercise

◯ _____   ◯ _____

☀ 3 Things ☀ to Remember for a New Day

1. Self-Care = Productivity

2. Self-Care = Self-Love

3. Alignment = Happiness

DATE: / /

TODAY I FELT:

○ **IN ALIGNMENT:**

What brought me inner joy and peace today?

_____

_____

_____

_____

○ **OUT OF ALIGNMENT:**

Did I do something that I did not connect with or made me feel unhappy? How can I start to change this?

_____

_____

_____

_____

TONIGHT I WILL FEED MY SOUL BY:

○ Learning something new   ○ Reading a book   ○ Getting creative

○ _____   ○ _____

TONIGHT'S MINDFULNESS PRACTICE WILL BE:

○ Yoga   ○ Meditation   ○ Exercise

○ _____   ○ _____

I Remain ONLY in the PRESENT Moment

TODAY I FELT:

○ **IN ALIGNMENT:**

What brought me inner joy and peace today?

_____

_____

_____

_____

○ **OUT OF ALIGNMENT:**

Did I do something that I did not connect with or made me feel
unhappy? How can I start to change this?

_____

_____

_____

_____

TONIGHT I WILL FEED MY SOUL BY:

○ Learning something new   ○ Reading a book   ○ Getting creative

○ _____   ○ _____

TONIGHT'S MINDFULNESS PRACTICE WILL BE:

○ Yoga   ○ Meditation   ○ Exercise

○ _____   ○ _____

WEEKLY CHECK-IN

Since you began your journey toward bringing more happiness and alignment into your life by using this journal, how do you think you have grown, no matter how big or small?

As growth can often be very gradual, when looking back you will be surprised by how much you have achieved. This question therefore not only helps to remind you of the power that you possess to grow but also gives you a moment to be proud of yourself.

Writing your achievement down will also help to solidify the idea in your mind that you can overcome any challenge that you set out to.

✳ SACRED SPACE ✳

Reflect on your week, set intentions for the next, make notes, or free-flow journal.

TODAY I FELT:

○ **IN ALIGNMENT:**

What brought me inner joy and peace today?

_____

_____

_____

_____

○ **OUT OF ALIGNMENT:**

Did I do something that I did not connect with or made me feel
unhappy? How can I start to change this?

_____

_____

_____

_____

TONIGHT I WILL FEED MY SOUL BY:

○ Learning something new   ○ Reading a book   ○ Getting creative

○ _____   ○ _____

TONIGHT'S MINDFULNESS PRACTICE WILL BE:

○ Yoga   ○ Meditation   ○ Exercise

○ _____   ○ _____

I AM DEEPLY CONNECTED TO MY MIND, BODY, AND SOUL

TODAY I FELT:

◯ **IN ALIGNMENT:**

What brought me inner joy and peace today?

_____

_____

_____

_____

◯ **OUT OF ALIGNMENT:**

Did I do something that I did not connect with or made me feel
unhappy? How can I start to change this?

_____

_____

_____

_____

TONIGHT I WILL FEED MY SOUL BY:

◯ Learning something new   ◯ Reading a book   ◯ Getting creative

◯ _____   ◯ _____

TONIGHT'S MINDFULNESS PRACTICE WILL BE:

◯ Yoga   ◯ Meditation   ◯ Exercise

◯ _____   ◯ _____

AS I GROW I GIVE MYSELF

PATIENCE AND GRACE

DATE: / /

TODAY I FELT:

○ **IN ALIGNMENT:**

What brought me inner joy and peace today?

_____

_____

_____

_____

○ **OUT OF ALIGNMENT:**

Did I do something that I did not connect with or made me feel
unhappy? How can I start to change this?

_____

_____

_____

_____

TONIGHT I WILL FEED MY SOUL BY:

○ Learning something new   ○ Reading a book   ○ Getting creative

○ _____   ○ _____

TONIGHT'S MINDFULNESS PRACTICE WILL BE:

○ Yoga   ○ Meditation   ○ Exercise

○ _____   ○ _____

4
Self-Care
Ideas

♥ Find a guided meditation for an area that you would like to work on, such as calming anxiety or manifestation

♥ Unwind in a bath with relaxing essential oils

♥ Listen to your favorite music

♥ Declutter your home—a tidy space can provide room for the clarity that your mind needs to thrive

TODAY I FELT:

○ **IN ALIGNMENT:**

What brought me inner joy and peace today?

_____

_____

_____

_____

○ **OUT OF ALIGNMENT:**

Did I do something that I did not connect with or made me feel
unhappy? How can I start to change this?

_____

_____

_____

_____

TONIGHT I WILL FEED MY SOUL BY:

○ Learning something new   ○ Reading a book   ○ Getting creative

○ _____   ○ _____

TONIGHT'S MINDFULNESS PRACTICE WILL BE:

○ Yoga   ○ Meditation   ○ Exercise

○ _____   ○ _____

I live with intention and follow my inner guidance wherever it may lead

TODAY I FELT:

○ **IN ALIGNMENT:**

What brought me inner joy and peace today?

_____

_____

_____

_____

○ **OUT OF ALIGNMENT:**

Did I do something that I did not connect with or made me feel
unhappy? How can I start to change this?

_____

_____

_____

_____

TONIGHT I WILL FEED MY SOUL BY:

○ Learning something new   ○ Reading a book   ○ Getting creative

○ _____   ○ _____

TONIGHT'S MINDFULNESS PRACTICE WILL BE:

○ Yoga   ○ Meditation   ○ Exercise

○ _____   ○ _____

WEEKLY CHECK-IN

List 15 things that make you happy.

This is a chance to remember the things that you may have forgotten about or haven't made time for lately.

✷ SACRED SPACE ✷

Reflect on your week, set intentions for the next, make notes, or free-flow journal.

TODAY I FELT:

○ **IN ALIGNMENT:**

What brought me inner joy and peace today?

_____

_____

_____

_____

○ **OUT OF ALIGNMENT:**

Did I do something that I did not connect with or made me feel
unhappy? How can I start to change this?

_____

_____

_____

_____

TONIGHT I WILL FEED MY SOUL BY:

○ Learning something new   ○ Reading a book   ○ Getting creative

○ _____   ○ _____

TONIGHT'S MINDFULNESS PRACTICE WILL BE:

○ Yoga   ○ Meditation   ○ Exercise

○ _____   ○ _____

I CHOOSE
♥ JOY ♥

TODAY I FELT:

◯ **IN ALIGNMENT:**

What brought me inner joy and peace today?

_____

_____

_____

_____

◯ **OUT OF ALIGNMENT:**

Did I do something that I did not connect with or made me feel
unhappy? How can I start to change this?

_____

_____

_____

_____

TONIGHT I WILL FEED MY SOUL BY:

◯ Learning something new   ◯ Reading a book   ◯ Getting creative

◯ _____   ◯ _____

TONIGHT'S MINDFULNESS PRACTICE WILL BE:

◯ Yoga   ◯ Meditation   ◯ Exercise

◯ _____   ◯ _____

✳ **MINDFULNESS AFFIRMATION** ✳

I GIVE THANKS
FOR THIS PRESENT MOMENT

DATE: / /

TODAY I FELT:

◯ **IN ALIGNMENT:**

What brought me inner joy and peace today?

_____

_____

_____

_____

◯ **OUT OF ALIGNMENT:**

Did I do something that I did not connect with or made me feel
unhappy? How can I start to change this?

_____

_____

_____

_____

TONIGHT I WILL FEED MY SOUL BY:

◯ Learning something new   ◯ Reading a book   ◯ Getting creative

◯ _____   ◯ _____

TONIGHT'S MINDFULNESS PRACTICE WILL BE:

◯ Yoga   ◯ Meditation   ◯ Exercise

◯ _____   ◯ _____

3 Reasons to Meditate

 Helps you to connect to your deepest desires

 Allows you to refocus your energy

 In the silence you can tap into the answers that you already have

TODAY I FELT:

○ **IN ALIGNMENT:**

What brought me inner joy and peace today?

_____

_____

_____

_____

○ **OUT OF ALIGNMENT:**

Did I do something that I did not connect with or made me feel
unhappy? How can I start to change this?

_____

_____

_____

_____

TONIGHT I WILL FEED MY SOUL BY:

○ Learning something new   ○ Reading a book   ○ Getting creative

○ _____   ○ _____

TONIGHT'S MINDFULNESS PRACTICE WILL BE:

○ Yoga   ○ Meditation   ○ Exercise

○ _____   ○ _____

I have the power to create any reality that I want

TODAY I FELT:

○ **IN ALIGNMENT:**

What brought me inner joy and peace today?

_____

_____

_____

_____

○ **OUT OF ALIGNMENT:**

Did I do something that I did not connect with or made me feel
unhappy? How can I start to change this?

_____

_____

_____

_____

TONIGHT I WILL FEED MY SOUL BY:

○ Learning something new   ○ Reading a book   ○ Getting creative

○ _____   ○ _____

TONIGHT'S MINDFULNESS PRACTICE WILL BE:

○ Yoga   ○ Meditation   ○ Exercise

○ _____   ○ _____

WEEKLY CHECK-IN

Are there any habits that you would like to break?
If so, why would you like to break them and what can you replace them with?

This could be anything from choosing to reach for your journal in the morning instead of your phone to beating negative self-talk by replacing it with self-love affirmations.

✸ SACRED SPACE ✸

Reflect on your week, set intentions for the next, make notes, or free-flow journal.

TODAY I FELT:

○ **IN ALIGNMENT:**

What brought me inner joy and peace today?

_____

_____

_____

_____

○ **OUT OF ALIGNMENT:**

Did I do something that I did not connect with or made me feel
unhappy? How can I start to change this?

_____

_____

_____

_____

TONIGHT I WILL FEED MY SOUL BY:

○ Learning something new   ○ Reading a book   ○ Getting creative

○ _____   ○ _____

TONIGHT'S MINDFULNESS PRACTICE WILL BE:

○ Yoga   ○ Meditation   ○ Exercise

○ _____   ○ _____

♥ I show myself ♥ love every ♥ day ♥

TODAY I FELT:

◯ **IN ALIGNMENT:**

What brought me inner joy and peace today?

_____

_____

_____

_____

◯ **OUT OF ALIGNMENT:**

Did I do something that I did not connect with or made me feel
unhappy? How can I start to change this?

_____

_____

_____

_____

TONIGHT I WILL FEED MY SOUL BY:

◯ Learning something new   ◯ Reading a book   ◯ Getting creative

◯ _____   ◯ _____

TONIGHT'S MINDFULNESS PRACTICE WILL BE:

◯ Yoga   ◯ Meditation   ◯ Exercise

◯ _____   ◯ _____

I AM DEEPLY

CONNECTED TO MY INNER BEING

TODAY I FELT:

◯ **IN ALIGNMENT:**

What brought me inner joy and peace today?

_____

_____

_____

_____

◯ **OUT OF ALIGNMENT:**

Did I do something that I did not connect with or made me feel
unhappy? How can I start to change this?

_____

_____

_____

_____

TONIGHT I WILL FEED MY SOUL BY:

◯ Learning something new   ◯ Reading a book   ◯ Getting creative

◯ _____   ◯ _____

TONIGHT'S MINDFULNESS PRACTICE WILL BE:

◯ Yoga   ◯ Meditation   ◯ Exercise

◯ _____   ◯ _____

Whenever you feel stuck or lost, it's okay to pause.

Take the time instead to do something that feeds your soul and lights you up inside.

You will soon reunite with a positive flow of energy and uncover the answers you are looking for.

TODAY I FELT:

◯ **IN ALIGNMENT:**

What brought me inner joy and peace today?

_____

_____

_____

_____

◯ **OUT OF ALIGNMENT:**

Did I do something that I did not connect with or made me feel
unhappy? How can I start to change this?

_____

_____

_____

_____

TONIGHT I WILL FEED MY SOUL BY:

◯ Learning something new   ◯ Reading a book   ◯ Getting creative

◯ _____   ◯ _____

TONIGHT'S MINDFULNESS PRACTICE WILL BE:

◯ Yoga   ◯ Meditation   ◯ Exercise

◯ _____   ◯ _____

I KNOW
♥ WHAT ♥
I TRULY
DESIRE

TODAY I FELT:

○ **IN ALIGNMENT:**

What brought me inner joy and peace today?

_____

_____

_____

_____

○ **OUT OF ALIGNMENT:**

Did I do something that I did not connect with or made me feel unhappy? How can I start to change this?

_____

_____

_____

_____

TONIGHT I WILL FEED MY SOUL BY:

○ Learning something new   ○ Reading a book   ○ Getting creative

○ _____   ○ _____

TONIGHT'S MINDFULNESS PRACTICE WILL BE:

○ Yoga   ○ Meditation   ○ Exercise

○ _____   ○ _____

WEEKLY CHECK-IN

List 10 things that you love about yourself, and why.

✳ SACRED SPACE ✳

Reflect on your week, set intentions for the next, make notes, or free-flow journal.

TODAY I FELT:

◯ **IN ALIGNMENT:**

What brought me inner joy and peace today?

_____

_____

_____

_____

◯ **OUT OF ALIGNMENT:**

Did I do something that I did not connect with or made me feel
unhappy? How can I start to change this?

_____

_____

_____

_____

TONIGHT I WILL FEED MY SOUL BY:

◯ Learning something new   ◯ Reading a book   ◯ Getting creative

◯ _____   ◯ _____

TONIGHT'S MINDFULNESS PRACTICE WILL BE:

◯ Yoga   ◯ Meditation   ◯ Exercise

◯ _____   ◯ _____

I LET GO OF FEAR

AND SIMPLY

FOLLOW MY

HEART

TODAY I FELT:

◯ **IN ALIGNMENT:**

What brought me inner joy and peace today?

_____

_____

_____

_____

◯ **OUT OF ALIGNMENT:**

Did I do something that I did not connect with or made me feel
unhappy? How can I start to change this?

_____

_____

_____

_____

TONIGHT I WILL FEED MY SOUL BY:

◯ Learning something new   ◯ Reading a book   ◯ Getting creative

◯ _____   ◯ _____

TONIGHT'S MINDFULNESS PRACTICE WILL BE:

◯ Yoga   ◯ Meditation   ◯ Exercise

◯ _____   ◯ _____

ALL OF MY ENERGY IS HERE NOW, IN THIS BEAUTIFUL PRESENT MOMENT

DATE: / /

TODAY I FELT:

◯ **IN ALIGNMENT:**

What brought me inner joy and peace today?

_____

_____

_____

_____

◯ **OUT OF ALIGNMENT:**

Did I do something that I did not connect with or made me feel
unhappy? How can I start to change this?

_____

_____

_____

_____

TONIGHT I WILL FEED MY SOUL BY:

◯ Learning something new   ◯ Reading a book   ◯ Getting creative

◯ _____   ◯ _____

TONIGHT'S MINDFULNESS PRACTICE WILL BE:

◯ Yoga   ◯ Meditation   ◯ Exercise

◯ _____   ◯ _____

4 Acts of Self-Love

♥ Eat energizing whole foods

♥ Remember to treat yourself

♥ Travel somewhere alone for a deep self-discovery

♥ Expand your mind with a new language or a new skill

TODAY I FELT:

◯ **IN ALIGNMENT:**

What brought me inner joy and peace today?

_____

_____

_____

_____

◯ **OUT OF ALIGNMENT:**

Did I do something that I did not connect with or made me feel
unhappy? How can I start to change this?

_____

_____

_____

_____

TONIGHT I WILL FEED MY SOUL BY:

◯ Learning something new   ◯ Reading a book   ◯ Getting creative

◯ _____   ◯ _____

TONIGHT'S MINDFULNESS PRACTICE WILL BE:

◯ Yoga   ◯ Meditation   ◯ Exercise

◯ _____   ◯ _____

TRUST ✳ ✳ IN THE POWER OF FOLLOWING YOUR OWN PATH ✳

TODAY I FELT:

◯ **IN ALIGNMENT:**

What brought me inner joy and peace today?

_____

_____

_____

_____

◯ **OUT OF ALIGNMENT:**

Did I do something that I did not connect with or made me feel
unhappy? How can I start to change this?

_____

_____

_____

_____

TONIGHT I WILL FEED MY SOUL BY:

◯ Learning something new   ◯ Reading a book   ◯ Getting creative

◯ _____   ◯ _____

TONIGHT'S MINDFULNESS PRACTICE WILL BE:

◯ Yoga   ◯ Meditation   ◯ Exercise

◯ _____   ◯ _____

WEEKLY CHECK-IN

Note any challenges that have shown up recently and start to think about how you can conquer them.

✻ SACRED SPACE ✻

Reflect on your week, set intentions for the next, make notes, or free-flow journal.

TODAY I FELT:

◯ **IN ALIGNMENT:**

What brought me inner joy and peace today?

_____

_____

_____

_____

◯ **OUT OF ALIGNMENT:**

Did I do something that I did not connect with or made me feel
unhappy? How can I start to change this?

_____

_____

_____

_____

TONIGHT I WILL FEED MY SOUL BY:

◯ Learning something new   ◯ Reading a book   ◯ Getting creative

◯ _____   ◯ _____

TONIGHT'S MINDFULNESS PRACTICE WILL BE:

◯ Yoga   ◯ Meditation   ◯ Exercise

◯ _____   ◯ _____

※ **SELF-LOVE AFFIRMATION** ※

MY MIND AND BODY ✳ ARE ✳ STRONG

TODAY I FELT:

◯ IN ALIGNMENT:

What brought me inner joy and peace today?

_____

_____

_____

_____

◯ OUT OF ALIGNMENT:

Did I do something that I did not connect with or made me feel
unhappy? How can I start to change this?

_____

_____

_____

_____

TONIGHT I WILL FEED MY SOUL BY:

◯ Learning something new   ◯ Reading a book   ◯ Getting creative

◯ _____   ◯ _____

TONIGHT'S MINDFULNESS PRACTICE WILL BE:

◯ Yoga   ◯ Meditation   ◯ Exercise

◯ _____   ◯ _____

I can easily access the answers to my questions within

DATE: / /

TODAY I FELT:

○ **IN ALIGNMENT:**

What brought me inner joy and peace today?

_____

_____

_____

_____

○ **OUT OF ALIGNMENT:**

Did I do something that I did not connect with or made me feel
unhappy? How can I start to change this?

_____

_____

_____

_____

TONIGHT I WILL FEED MY SOUL BY:

○ Learning something new   ○ Reading a book   ○ Getting creative

○ _____   ○ _____

TONIGHT'S MINDFULNESS PRACTICE WILL BE:

○ Yoga   ○ Meditation   ○ Exercise

○ _____   ○ _____

3
Reasons
to Practice Gratitude

● When you practice it regularly, you will find that you are able to center yourself more effortlessly when you are going through a challenging time

🌙 It allows you to easily see the pure beauty and magic in every day

 You will clearly recognize the abundance that you already have

TODAY I FELT:

○ **IN ALIGNMENT:**

What brought me inner joy and peace today?

_____

_____

_____

_____

○ **OUT OF ALIGNMENT:**

Did I do something that I did not connect with or made me feel
unhappy? How can I start to change this?

_____

_____

_____

_____

TONIGHT I WILL FEED MY SOUL BY:

○ Learning something new   ○ Reading a book   ○ Getting creative

○ _____   ○ _____

TONIGHT'S MINDFULNESS PRACTICE WILL BE:

○ Yoga   ○ Meditation   ○ Exercise

○ _____   ○ _____

Self-Love
Is Embracing
Yourself
♥ **Fully** ♥
Just as You
Are

TODAY I FELT:

◯ **IN ALIGNMENT:**

What brought me inner joy and peace today?

_____

_____

_____

_____

◯ **OUT OF ALIGNMENT:**

Did I do something that I did not connect with or made me feel
unhappy? How can I start to change this?

_____

_____

_____

_____

TONIGHT I WILL FEED MY SOUL BY:

◯ Learning something new   ◯ Reading a book   ◯ Getting creative

◯ _____   ◯ _____

TONIGHT'S MINDFULNESS PRACTICE WILL BE:

◯ Yoga   ◯ Meditation   ◯ Exercise

◯ _____   ◯ _____

WEEKLY CHECK-IN

Who have you been grateful for this week, and why?

✳ SACRED SPACE ✳

Reflect on your week, set intentions for the next, make notes, or free-flow journal.

TODAY I FELT:

◯ **IN ALIGNMENT:**

What brought me inner joy and peace today?

_____

_____

_____

_____

◯ **OUT OF ALIGNMENT:**

Did I do something that I did not connect with or made me feel
unhappy? How can I start to change this?

_____

_____

_____

_____

TONIGHT I WILL FEED MY SOUL BY:

◯ Learning something new   ◯ Reading a book   ◯ Getting creative

◯ _____   ◯ _____

TONIGHT'S MINDFULNESS PRACTICE WILL BE:

◯ Yoga   ◯ Meditation   ◯ Exercise

◯ _____   ◯ _____

I hold the key to my happiness

TODAY I FELT:

◯ **IN ALIGNMENT:**

What brought me inner joy and peace today?

_____

_____

_____

_____

◯ **OUT OF ALIGNMENT:**

Did I do something that I did not connect with or made me feel
unhappy? How can I start to change this?

_____

_____

_____

_____

TONIGHT I WILL FEED MY SOUL BY:

◯ Learning something new   ◯ Reading a book   ◯ Getting creative

◯ _____   ◯ _____

TONIGHT'S MINDFULNESS PRACTICE WILL BE:

◯ Yoga   ◯ Meditation   ◯ Exercise

◯ _____   ◯ _____

TODAY I FELT:

◯ **IN ALIGNMENT:**

What brought me inner joy and peace today?

_____

_____

_____

_____

◯ **OUT OF ALIGNMENT:**

Did I do something that I did not connect with or made me feel
unhappy? How can I start to change this?

_____

_____

_____

_____

TONIGHT I WILL FEED MY SOUL BY:

◯ Learning something new   ◯ Reading a book   ◯ Getting creative

◯ _____   ◯ _____

TONIGHT'S MINDFULNESS PRACTICE WILL BE:

◯ Yoga   ◯ Meditation   ◯ Exercise

◯ _____   ◯ _____

3 Benefits of Meditation

 Helps you to get into your flow

 Allows you to reconnect with yourself

 Creates a calm and still space to practice gratitude

TODAY I FELT:

○ **IN ALIGNMENT:**

What brought me inner joy and peace today?

_____

_____

_____

_____

○ **OUT OF ALIGNMENT:**

Did I do something that I did not connect with or made me feel
unhappy? How can I start to change this?

_____

_____

_____

_____

TONIGHT I WILL FEED MY SOUL BY:

○ Learning something new   ○ Reading a book   ○ Getting creative

○ _____   ○ _____

TONIGHT'S MINDFULNESS PRACTICE WILL BE:

○ Yoga   ○ Meditation   ○ Exercise

○ _____   ○ _____

Once you make SELF-CARE your top priority, ABSOLUTELY anything is possible

TODAY I FELT:

◯ **IN ALIGNMENT:**

What brought me inner joy and peace today?

_____

_____

_____

_____

◯ **OUT OF ALIGNMENT:**

Did I do something that I did not connect with or made me feel
unhappy? How can I start to change this?

_____

_____

_____

_____

TONIGHT I WILL FEED MY SOUL BY:

◯ Learning something new   ◯ Reading a book   ◯ Getting creative

◯ _____   ◯ _____

TONIGHT'S MINDFULNESS PRACTICE WILL BE:

◯ Yoga   ◯ Meditation   ◯ Exercise

◯ _____   ◯ _____

WEEKLY CHECK-IN

Are there any things that you have been meaning to try but have maybe not found the time for yet?

Use this section to write a plan of action, and if next week is not feasible, set a date/time frame that you will stick to.

✳ SACRED SPACE ✳

Reflect on your week, set intentions for the next, make notes, or free-flow journal.

TODAY I FELT:

◯ IN ALIGNMENT:

What brought me inner joy and peace today?

_____

_____

_____

_____

◯ OUT OF ALIGNMENT:

Did I do something that I did not connect with or made me feel
unhappy? How can I start to change this?

_____

_____

_____

_____

TONIGHT I WILL FEED MY SOUL BY:

◯ Learning something new   ◯ Reading a book   ◯ Getting creative

◯ _____   ◯ _____

TONIGHT'S MINDFULNESS PRACTICE WILL BE:

◯ Yoga   ◯ Meditation   ◯ Exercise

◯ _____   ◯ _____

I let self-care enrich my daily life

TODAY I FELT:

○ **IN ALIGNMENT:**

What brought me inner joy and peace today?

_____

_____

_____

_____

○ **OUT OF ALIGNMENT:**

Did I do something that I did not connect with or made me feel
unhappy? How can I start to change this?

_____

_____

_____

_____

TONIGHT I WILL FEED MY SOUL BY:

○ Learning something new   ○ Reading a book   ○ Getting creative

○ _____   ○ _____

TONIGHT'S MINDFULNESS PRACTICE WILL BE:

○ Yoga   ○ Meditation   ○ Exercise

○ _____   ○ _____

I HONOR MYSELF

AND FOLLOW MY INNER VOICE WHEREVER IT MAY LEAD

TODAY I FELT:

○ **IN ALIGNMENT:**

What brought me inner joy and peace today?

_____

_____

_____

_____

○ **OUT OF ALIGNMENT:**

Did I do something that I did not connect with or made me feel
unhappy? How can I start to change this?

_____

_____

_____

_____

TONIGHT I WILL FEED MY SOUL BY:

○ Learning something new   ○ Reading a book   ○ Getting creative

○ _____   ○ _____

TONIGHT'S MINDFULNESS PRACTICE WILL BE:

○ Yoga   ○ Meditation   ○ Exercise

○ _____   ○ _____

4 Acts of Self-Love

♥ Follow your passion

♥ Listen to your intuition

♥ Practice learning to let go of the
energy that no longer serves you

♥ Be confidently you—you are magical!

TODAY I FELT:

◯ **IN ALIGNMENT:**

What brought me inner joy and peace today?

_____

_____

_____

_____

◯ **OUT OF ALIGNMENT:**

Did I do something that I did not connect with or made me feel
unhappy? How can I start to change this?

_____

_____

_____

_____

TONIGHT I WILL FEED MY SOUL BY:

◯ Learning something new   ◯ Reading a book   ◯ Getting creative

◯ _____   ◯ _____

TONIGHT'S MINDFULNESS PRACTICE WILL BE:

◯ Yoga   ◯ Meditation   ◯ Exercise

◯ _____   ◯ _____

I take the time to sit with my emotions to uncover  MY TRUTH

TODAY I FELT:

◯ IN ALIGNMENT:

What brought me inner joy and peace today?

_____

_____

_____

_____

◯ OUT OF ALIGNMENT:

Did I do something that I did not connect with or made me feel
unhappy? How can I start to change this?

_____

_____

_____

_____

TONIGHT I WILL FEED MY SOUL BY:

◯ Learning something new   ◯ Reading a book   ◯ Getting creative

◯ _____   ◯ _____

TONIGHT'S MINDFULNESS PRACTICE WILL BE:

◯ Yoga   ◯ Meditation   ◯ Exercise

◯ _____   ◯ _____

WEEKLY CHECK-IN

How would you like to grow next week?

Use this space to set a challenge for yourself. This could be personal
or work related. All growth is deeply rewarding, so this challenge
can be as grand or as seemingly small as you would like.

✳ SACRED SPACE ✳

Reflect on your week, set intentions for the next, make notes, or free-flow journal.

TODAY I FELT:

○ **IN ALIGNMENT:**

What brought me inner joy and peace today?

_____

_____

_____

_____

○ **OUT OF ALIGNMENT:**

Did I do something that I did not connect with or made me feel
unhappy? How can I start to change this?

_____

_____

_____

_____

TONIGHT I WILL FEED MY SOUL BY:

○ Learning something new   ○ Reading a book   ○ Getting creative

○ _____   ○ _____

TONIGHT'S MINDFULNESS PRACTICE WILL BE:

○ Yoga   ○ Meditation   ○ Exercise

○ _____   ○ _____

I Love Who ♥ I Am ♥

TODAY I FELT:

◯ **IN ALIGNMENT:**

What brought me inner joy and peace today?

_____

_____

_____

_____

◯ **OUT OF ALIGNMENT:**

Did I do something that I did not connect with or made me feel
unhappy? How can I start to change this?

_____

_____

_____

_____

TONIGHT I WILL FEED MY SOUL BY:

◯ Learning something new   ◯ Reading a book   ◯ Getting creative

◯ _____   ◯ _____

TONIGHT'S MINDFULNESS PRACTICE WILL BE:

◯ Yoga   ◯ Meditation   ◯ Exercise

◯ _____   ◯ _____

REMEMBER TO SPEND

TIME IN GROUNDING
NATURE

TODAY I FELT:

○ **IN ALIGNMENT:**

What brought me inner joy and peace today?

_____

_____

_____

_____

○ **OUT OF ALIGNMENT:**

Did I do something that I did not connect with or made me feel
unhappy? How can I start to change this?

_____

_____

_____

_____

TONIGHT I WILL FEED MY SOUL BY:

○ Learning something new ○ Reading a book ○ Getting creative

○ _____ ○ _____

TONIGHT'S MINDFULNESS PRACTICE WILL BE:

○ Yoga ○ Meditation ○ Exercise

○ _____ ○ _____

I can easily tap into peaceful energy

TODAY I FELT:

○ **IN ALIGNMENT:**

What brought me inner joy and peace today?

_____

_____

_____

_____

○ **OUT OF ALIGNMENT:**

Did I do something that I did not connect with or made me feel
unhappy? How can I start to change this?

_____

_____

_____

_____

TONIGHT I WILL FEED MY SOUL BY:

○ Learning something new   ○ Reading a book   ○ Getting creative

○ _____   ○ _____

TONIGHT'S MINDFULNESS PRACTICE WILL BE:

○ Yoga   ○ Meditation   ○ Exercise

○ _____   ○ _____

BELIEVE YOU CAN AND YOU WILL

TODAY I FELT:

DATE: / /

○ **IN ALIGNMENT:**

What brought me inner joy and peace today?

_____

_____

_____

_____

○ **OUT OF ALIGNMENT:**

Did I do something that I did not connect with or made me feel unhappy? How can I start to change this?

_____

_____

_____

_____

TONIGHT I WILL FEED MY SOUL BY:

○ Learning something new   ○ Reading a book   ○ Getting creative

○ _____   ○ _____

TONIGHT'S MINDFULNESS PRACTICE WILL BE:

○ Yoga   ○ Meditation   ○ Exercise

○ _____   ○ _____

WEEKLY CHECK-IN

**Are there any new habits that you would like to create
that you think will enrich your life?**

Use the section below to think about how and when you could
start implementing them.

✳ SACRED SPACE ✳

Reflect on your week, set intentions for the next, make notes, or free-flow journal.

TODAY I FELT:

○ **IN ALIGNMENT:**

What brought me inner joy and peace today?

_____

_____

_____

_____

○ **OUT OF ALIGNMENT:**

Did I do something that I did not connect with or made me feel
unhappy? How can I start to change this?

_____

_____

_____

_____

TONIGHT I WILL FEED MY SOUL BY:

○ Learning something new   ○ Reading a book   ○ Getting creative

○ _____   ○ _____

TONIGHT'S MINDFULNESS PRACTICE WILL BE:

○ Yoga   ○ Meditation   ○ Exercise

○ _____   ○ _____

YOU ARE MAGIC

DATE: / /

TODAY I FELT:

○ **IN ALIGNMENT:**

What brought me inner joy and peace today?

_____

_____

_____

_____

○ **OUT OF ALIGNMENT:**

Did I do something that I did not connect with or made me feel
unhappy? How can I start to change this?

_____

_____

_____

_____

TONIGHT I WILL FEED MY SOUL BY:

○ Learning something new   ○ Reading a book   ○ Getting creative

○ _____   ○ _____

TONIGHT'S MINDFULNESS PRACTICE WILL BE:

○ Yoga   ○ Meditation   ○ Exercise

○ _____   ○ _____

I CAN
EASILY
ACCESS
✳ MY ✳
POWERS

TODAY I FELT:

◯ **IN ALIGNMENT:**

What brought me inner joy and peace today?

_____

_____

_____

_____

◯ **OUT OF ALIGNMENT:**

Did I do something that I did not connect with or made me feel
unhappy? How can I start to change this?

_____

_____

_____

_____

TONIGHT I WILL FEED MY SOUL BY:

◯ Learning something new   ◯ Reading a book   ◯ Getting creative

◯ _____   ◯ _____

TONIGHT'S MINDFULNESS PRACTICE WILL BE:

◯ Yoga   ◯ Meditation   ◯ Exercise

◯ _____   ◯ _____

I LET GO OF ALL THAT I CANNOT CONTROL

AND REMAIN AT ONE WITH MY PEACEFUL INNER BEING

TODAY I FELT:

◯ **IN ALIGNMENT:**

What brought me inner joy and peace today?

_____

_____

_____

_____

◯ **OUT OF ALIGNMENT:**

Did I do something that I did not connect with or made me feel
unhappy? How can I start to change this?

_____

_____

_____

_____

TONIGHT I WILL FEED MY SOUL BY:

◯ Learning something new   ◯ Reading a book   ◯ Getting creative

◯ _____   ◯ _____

TONIGHT'S MINDFULNESS PRACTICE WILL BE:

◯ Yoga   ◯ Meditation   ◯ Exercise

◯ _____   ◯ _____

I flow
confidently
with
my own
energy

TODAY I FELT:

○ **IN ALIGNMENT:**

What brought me inner joy and peace today?

_____

_____

_____

_____

○ **OUT OF ALIGNMENT:**

Did I do something that I did not connect with or made me feel
unhappy? How can I start to change this?

_____

_____

_____

_____

TONIGHT I WILL FEED MY SOUL BY:

○ Learning something new   ○ Reading a book   ○ Getting creative

○ _____   ○ _____

TONIGHT'S MINDFULNESS PRACTICE WILL BE:

○ Yoga   ○ Meditation   ○ Exercise

○ _____   ○ _____

I am wholeheartedly connected ♥ to this ♥ present moment

✳ ABOUT THE AUTHOR ✳

Photograph of the author by Joanne Crawford

Kelsey Layne is a designer and self-confessed journal/stationery lover. As the founder of Note and Shine, she is bringing her vision of beautifully designed, user-friendly journals and paper products into the world, including *The Manifestation Journal* and *The Self-Love Journal*. She lives in York, England.

tarcherperigee

An imprint of Penguin Random House LLC
penguinrandomhouse.com

TarcherPerigee with tp colophon is a registered trademark of Penguin Random House LLC.

Most TarcherPerigee books are available at special quantity discounts for bulk purchase for sales promotions, premiums, fund-raising, and educational needs. Special books or book excerpts also can be created to fit specific needs. For details, write SpecialMarkets@penguinrandomhouse.com.

Trade paperback ISBN: 9780593543627

Printed in the United States of America
1st Printing

Book design by Kelsey Layne